one man's trash

matt chamberlain + spreken

First published in 2017 by
Wordsmithery
5 Curzon Road
Chatham
Kent, ME4 5ST
www.wordsmithery.info

Copyright © 2017 Matt Chamberlain and Spreken.

The right of Matt Chamberlain and Spreken to be identified as the authors of this work has been asserted by them in accordance with Section 77 of the Copyright, Design and Patents Act 1988.

All rights reserved. Requests to reproduce the text in any format should be addressed to the publisher. No reproduction of any part of this book may take place, whether stored in a retrieval system, or transmitted in any form, by any means, electronic, mechanical, photocopying, recording or otherwise, without prior permission from Wordsmithery.

This is a work of fiction. All characters appearing in this work, other than those in the public domain, are fictitious, and any resemblance to real persons, living or dead, is purely coincidental.

A CIP record for this book is available from the British Library.

This book is sold subject to the conditions it shall not, by way of trade or otherwise, be lent, re-sold, hired out, or otherwise circulated without the publisher's prior consent in any form or binding or cover other than that in which it is published and without a similar condition including this condition being imposed on the subsequent purchaser.

isbn 978-0-9926853-6-2
printed in Great Britain on recycled paper
by Inky Little Fingers

Foreword

Spreken and Matt Chamberlain were fans of each other's work. They got talking. They saw parallels. Each thought the other an economical poet; each participated fitfully in the Medway poetry scene; each displayed fluctuating motivation. They both also recognised that fluency in expressing sadness could easily become a form of poetic self-harm. A gear change was needed and the lit-art project, *An Assemblance of Judicious Heretics*, showed them the way.

They noted that this exhibition and live performance event, which anonymously pairs writers and visual artists, essentially forces collaboration upon the solitary.

They appreciated the fresh perspectives created when an artist interprets a mystery writer's words.

They wondered about doing this the other way round, each writing based on an image supplied by the other. And if the images – offered with no explanation – were deliberately boring, random, unspecific or grim, and their interpreter's only remit was to see something positive in them, this would be poetically exciting.

It was decided. This is how they would emerge from the corners they'd written themselves into.

One man's trash is another man's treasure. Or hope. Or mirth. It could be all sorts of things, but for the co-authors of this book, it has been a pleasure.

Contents

Picasso's crystal gems	2
Speak not of waste	5
How many hearts?	6
Lifeblood	8
United circle	10
Underneath	13
Some old mission	14
Patchwork	17
Grey infusion	18
Missing the point	20
Beauty in a bin bag	22
Free	25
I made my mark	26
Leading lady	29
About the authors	33

Picasso's crystal gems

Picasso's crystal gems

They usually whitewash dead shop windows
to make you think they have something worth hiding.
But not this one; it shouts that there's nothing to see.
Forget me, forget me, forget me!
You're only a shop if you've something to sell
and this concern's neither going
nor even of any concern
to any of the passers-by who do just that.
Forget, forget abandoned cavern
of biker oddments which nobody bought
even back then, when helmets were billiard balls
and at your own risk.
No further transactions;
it's only for looking, and not even that.

But irrelevance takes the pressure off
memories turn filigree once they're forgotten.
Forget, forget and bring to life a stricken window:
procreating sunlight shards;
cubist portal,
silent sigh,
museum of jewels,
it is Picasso's glitter-ball.
When average days
drip middling light
the fracture forks
and branches like streetlamps viewed through tears,
dispersing,
reaching,
luscious lux,
a twilight trinket

copper oxide collage,
humming heady claret notes
and rings of soda lime.
Forgotten, neglected,
misplaced shapes now cosied up,
joined at the hip;
if one falls they all fall –
kaleidoscopic unity;
haphazard shards, they have no downside.
No risk, no disadvantage.

No refunds, no complaints.
Elapsed merchant with nothing to sell.
Forget, forget!
The loveliness of being forgotten:
in broken glass, Picasso's crystal gems.

And woman with dog,
and small packet of dog shit –
well, she could walk another way to her wherever,
but chooses this way
on each and every day
and always takes notice
and always remembers
that there is no need for whitewash
when unfit helmet is at your own risk;
and, though she sighs at the basket
of somebody's memories,
she smiles like the open road
and basks in Pablo's diamonds
free of charge.

Speak not of waste

Speak not of waste

Speak not of waste,
For I see none.

Contained within the cycle of this now decaying orb,
A different tale indeed.

Crisp morning air, glitter on grass;
Shimmering snow and crunch underfoot;
The muffled whispers of secret lovers.
Howling wind, waterfall clouds in silver sky;
The gentle kiss of sun's first warmth.
Pure, unfaltering heat; cloudless blue above,
Scorched golden-brown below.

Unhurried, uninterrupted.
Undisturbed, fruition reached;
Surpassed.

Minutiae so generously fed.
Time after time.
Meal after meal.
Day after day.
An endless banquet for the butterfly's ball.

And in completion, the wheel turns.
These magical spheres disperse,
Disappear beneath;
To return in spirit to their inception,
And bring forth new life from within.

Speak not of waste.
For there is none.

How many hearts?

Roll

and smoulder slow;

slow-cooker breathe faint succour in slack silver curls.

Minutes are asset bubbles

so rumble and drip,

linger, persist and

blip . . .

blip . . .

blip. . .

But time's rant is life's rave, and tick tick mule kick microwave screams out as Russell Hobbs's time-bomb glowers, tick tick tick. . . Now move it, quick! Later than late, and three-minute shrill is finished under the grill, and stack your plate for later, change that water, let it soak, put that down and go! Coats on, shoes on, lid off, stir it. . . Tick tick tick of micro days in ceaseless waves and leave it, move it, tick tick DING! Are we there yet?

Are we back yet? Welcome party: two beers, one glass, seven plates, two bowls, one jug, five mugs – what kind of rebel maths is that? But ask them, how many hearts? How many mouths producing notes that fuse to make how many harmonies?

When knives all point the same way and mayhems track a mutual aim, then love is tallied in tick, tick, tick, and

time

proves

in that giant mixing bowl –

a complex dough of brilliant red with violet notes:

one part hurt, eight parts comfort,

steeped in smirks, glugs of laughter,

and every restful courtesy,

all

home made.

Lifeblood

Timeless beauty, interrupted,
Bespoiled, I say.

The trees whisper, look closer:

Constant motion.
Forward, always forward.
Past happenings do not hinder,
Yet to come does not concern.

Discarded remnants of others' misdeeds
Swept along, washed clean, in time
Broken down, and disappear.

Barriers do not halt it –
Merely pause, and find a new direction;
But onward. Always onward
To fate's destination.

Symbol of peace, this gentle river,
Power unknown hidden deep.
Dirtied maybe, for a time.
For time will heal.

Lifeblood of the earth.
Coursing forth.
Unyielding.
Unspoiled.

Lifeblood

United circle

I "seem to see
the river Tiber foaming"
with much puke.
Contrast frightens; strangers spook;

so nauseate, create the dismal
scorch and scar dim white supremacy.
His legacy?
Angry smear; dark veto daub;

Oh, Big Splash Lad.

And yet that hate just will not bloody integrate;
stays with its own,
spray-painted into ghetto corner.
One man
pointing manly can,

uncertain what he wants to ban. . .
. . . but someone has to "say it like it is"
and the voice of reason
it is his?

Things were fine before the strangers.

Today the sun's out and so's the word
so here we come
and (uninvited) still we come
to stand
and to answer men
who long to be The Man.
The free crowd forms while cornered rat
can only let the paint do the talking
but, as he runs, "No blacks!" he cries
into ever brightening skies.

See that angry shape you drew?
Four-legged symbol Nazis slew?
I seem to see a Catherine wheel
which, like these people, runs fine rings round you –
single sparks that fuse, to form
united circles.
You know, like strangers do.

Underneath

Underneath

Who's that trip-trapping across my bridge?

A pair of heels in a hurry,
smart suit,
but furrowed brow and blistered heel.
Time is not her friend today,
wish away these last few hours
to wine and fireside.

Wellies and wheels,
trainers trail behind,
catching the slipstream of boundless energy.
Wearied days lead to restless nights,
treasure these moments of noise and movement,
for between bedtime and breakfast there is nothing.

Thick soled black boots,
slow thud of uneven step,
gentle clink of chain and buckle.
Armour plated image, carefully created,
hides a reality that cannot ask her
if she'd like to go for a drink.

Smart dress shoes,
well worn but shining,
shuffling steadily homeward.
No-one but the cat now awaits his arrival –
warm silk slip around the shins,
soft-sound relief at his return.

Down here in the still,
troll's eye view alters perception.
Dull concrete slabs are but the needles
that knit all threads together.
Plain design the canvas
for life to daub its colours upon.

Some old mission

Bolt some place,
abscond somewhere,
escape suspicion?

Advance somehow,
explore something,
forge tradition?

Or indulging,
meeting, what,
human condition?

Goals, poles apart;
headway in straight lines.

Point one way – no-one to direct them.

Slash the dark;
regimented lamps' coronas.

Light undying – no-one to extinguish them.

Murmur chords;
wheels all sing

the same note – no-one to conduct them.

Directionless and improvised,
permanent habitual,
monotone and sundry

yet every one
has someone to see;
has something to flee;
has a universal need to be

somewhere.

Some old mission

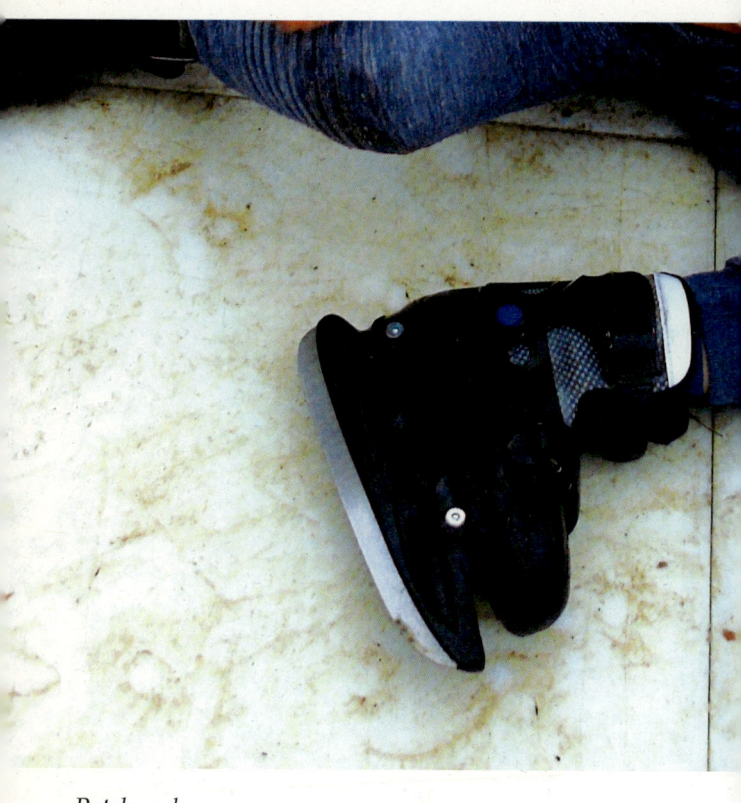

Patchwork

Patchwork

Pigeon steps tap tap tap,
accompanying head nod
and concentration tongue.

Hasty zigzag,
frantic panic –
do not look up.

Symbiotic swirls of aesthetic perfection,
paint on smiles and spray on hair.
Do not look down.

None so perfect to leave no trace,
all your secrets are here.
Tap tap tap – glide – tap tap;

Zigzag gives way to train track;
Symbiosis broken briefly,
a wobble in that flawless spiral.

Ah! And see: a great wide sweep.
Mine is not the only fall from grace.

Down here, at the root of it all,
every one of us balanced precariously
on implausibly thin foundations.

Dirty patchwork tells a tale.
You are not alone.

Grey infusion

Well excuse ME!
Don't mind me, love –
I'm just a scruffy little pigeon
in a grubby little puddle.
But your unstable jumble-mob,
all knees and elbows,
you're all just making dust;
scuttledizzy jostlers;
sidestepping my al fresco ashtray.
Pull up a pause, mate! Have a quench!
Grey infusion
puts a fizz in little steps;
frost-cool trickle
stroking prickly throat.
I wear my oil slick round my neck;
you peel parched,
dried out with rage and toil
groping London haste.
And you call ME feral!

Rush on by, son, caked in tension;
curdled morning's sticking
to your scrabbled rapid limbs.
I bet you didn't know the breeze
could peck and smooch.
Slap a bit of this on.
Suits me, don't it? Oi!
Watch where you're standing!
Grit-scrub rouses sheer skin –
the earth has bubbles;
rubber duck as scrubby pigeon;
cleanliness is next to calmness.

Slow down, darlin', it's bottlenecking.
Skirting round a murky hindrance
that's clear as millet to me;
I delve right in – it doesn't mind.
I agitate
a polished surface;
stamp to find out
where the bottom is.
You lot should try it.
Kick it 'cause it's there;
bathe wildly; drowsy gulps; splash-dance;
Take it neat.

Missing the point

Pay here
Queue there
Stop this
Do that
Wait here
Walk there
Red light
Green light
Drive here
Park there
Buy this
Watch that

Look for the signs.

Look up.

See?

Until they can put up a sign
telling that great expanse of blue
how to behave,
they control nothing.

Missing the point

Beauty in a bin bag

Burly bouncer –
shiny Puffa jacketed,
black duvet bound
all tar marshmallow –
guards exclusive nite-spot;
high-class, steep,
gated both ends;
throb-tunes rattle;
fashionistas pay for features;
glasses clink, and
fresh tunes clank like blades;
narrow dancefloor goes well deep.

He hangs here in wide old daylight, too,
leaning on the lacquered bar
glorious in its azure trim.
There is no dark to
glisten in, but he glows ebony
in weightless light.
Jet pillow-man is daytime's night;
beams of shade
that brighten pasty vistas.

He's lured here
by the charm of silhouette;
he stays here when they've all crawled home –
if there's no shadow, you're not there.
But he is here, in crumpled beauty;
breezes ripple jutting muscle;
he throws shapes
in crude oil spotlights.
It's what some people call

Security.

Beauty in a bin bag

Free

Free

Muddied boots.
Another chore to add to the list
upon your return.
Clean, polish, buff, dubbin –
Ready to walk again.

It is nothing special,
this magical place.
Fields, walls, trees.
The occasional daisy, maybe.

It costs nothing,
this invaluable space.
Grab a coat, flask of coffee.
Pull on your boots.

Time out here is sacred.
As a call to prayer draws some,
this space draws you.

For as you walk,
ankle deep in memories and talk,
it all stays behind;
left at the boundary of that last field.

It'll be waiting for you.

But right now,
you're free.

I made my mark

Strapping blond medieval scaffold,
a single-finger tent pole:
hoisting up all ancient triumphs;
spires aspiring monumental;
stained-glass heft and marvel, seeks
the eyes to find its light;
turret glories, mezzo fresco;
low-glow bells lick descant brasses;
gargoyles, effigies, apostles;
ageless thunder-pipes;
all within the milky pillars
plundered, desecrated, yet restored,
ledger stones for the elite.

And yet that's my mark;
X to mark a spot where,
through one thousand years and fashions,
common people came to worship;
lower orders, fears and fealty,
destitution, hope and safety,
and a roof made by my hands.
We mislaid lives in this construction, but
we are remembered, too –
not like those in rousing murals
but in small graffiti-kisses.
We're long-dead now but see what we made;
look what we raised up to heaven.

Hosts of worthies;
countless epochs;
but there's my little mark.

I made my mark

Leading lady

Leading lady

There were birds here just now.
A car door slammed.
Now they're gone.

I am here for now.
One day a wooden box will slam.
I'll be gone.

It is too easy to feel there is no time
To do enough, to see enough, to be enough.
Cram your days with new sights,
travel the world in search of new experiences,
and not even have seen or done one single percent
of all the things that exist under this same sky.
But there are worlds within worlds.
And plays within plays.

In mum-world, I am the queen, the president,
the mayor, and the greatest scholar who ever lived;
while simultaneously the cook, the maid, the teacher,
and all the civil servants.

There is the sitcom about the dancer,
with her busy social life and endless performance schedule.
I'm top of the credits roll in that.

I nightly perform that famous monologue
about the woman walking her dog.

The beautiful play about the lonely single woman
who is rescued from the confines of her own depressive mind
and learns what love is.
That one had my name in lights.

And when one day I get that final curtain call,
that inevitable encore-less bow that comes to us all,
And they ask me "What did you DO with your life?
Did you feel the chill of an arctic sunrise?
Invent a way of recycling old shoes into clean fuel?
See the view from the top of the Eiffel Tower?
Swim with a dolphin?
Freefall from 30,000 feet?"
I shall say, with hand on heart :
"I played my part,
I played my part."

Poems by Spreken based on photos by Matt Chamberlain

Speak not of waste
Lifeblood
Underneath*
Patchwork
Missing the point
Free
Leading lady

Poems by Matt Chamberlain based on photos by Spreken

Picasso's crystal gems*
How many hearts?
United circle
Some old mission
Grey infusion
Beauty in a bin bag
I made my mark

* Previously published in *Confluence* (Wordsmithery), February 2017

Cover image by Matt Chamberlain.

About the authors

SPREKEN has been writing poetry since she was sixteen and won honorary membership of the Poetry Society for one of her competition entries. One of her poems gained one of the coveted displays on the London Underground. She has had work published in *An Assemblance of Judicious Heretics* (Wordsmithery) and co-headlined Paint It Black, a poetry event focusing on mental health, as part of Medway's Paint the Town festival in 2017.

MATT CHAMBERLAIN has published three poetry collections (for details see www.mattchamberlainpoe.wix.com/poetry) and has contributed writing to *Confluence* magazine, *An Assemblance of Judicious Heretics* (Wordsmithery), the *Magnolia Review* and Wandering Words. He has performed his work regularly at festivals, literary events, charity gigs and open mic nights in Kent and London. He is the 2017 Vicar's Picnic Festival Laureate.

Wordsmithery is a Medway-based independent literary arts organisation which specialises in managing literature events and projects, Literature Development, and publishing. **www.wordsmithery.info**

Check out our limited edition books: Poetry and prose

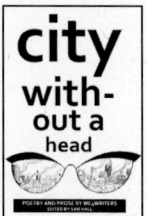

City without a head
ISBN: 978-0-9926853-0-0 Paperback, 156pp, October 2013, £12
Writings by: B Fentiman; S Hall (ed); SM Jenkin; AM Jordan; S March; T Moyle; R Smith. Ink drawings by V Wainwright
A collection of poetry and prose taking the format of an alphabetical index. '... *an exceptionally refreshing and eloquent anthology.*' **** FemaleArts

An assemblance of judicious heretics
ISBN: 978-0-9926853-3-1 Paperback, 100pp, full colour illustrations October 2015, £15
This beautiful illustrated anthology documents a large scale collaborative project from literary and visual artists from Medway and beyond. 32 writers and 35 artists' work is showcased in the book.
'...*an important snapshot of what was happening in the Medway literary and arts scene...*'

The Unbearable Sheerness of Being
by Barry Fentiman Hall
Paperback, 32pp, 2016, £5
From scorpions, and overheard teenagers, to an escaped dog and an encounter with a timeless entity, follow in BFH's fantastical footsteps as he travels round the island in this collection of poems and a story.

Beautiful Monsters
by Sam Hall
Paperback, 36pp, 2017, £6
Six short stories putting modern slant on the notion of fairytales. Magical curses, parallel dimensions, ghostly encounters, devilish fashion, and friendly giant spiders. The cover of each copy of *Beautiful Monsters* is hand-printed, so each copy is unique.

Check out our limited edition books: Plays

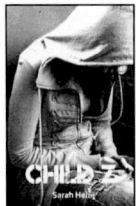

Child Z by Sarah Hehir
ISBN: 978-0-9926853-1-7 Paperback, 56pp, June 2015, £9.99
Child Z by award-winning playwright Sarah Hehir, is a hard hitting new play which gives voice to a young girl trapped at the centre of a child grooming ring. Powerful, provocative and timely. *'... a play that is every bit as moving as it is necessary.'* ***** FemaleArts

Zero Down by Sarah Hehir
ISBN: 978-0-9926853-2-4 Paperback, 60pp, August 2015, £9.99
Zero Down takes you into the life of the late shift at a rundown nursing home: a night of dubious dreams, subterfuge, aggression and betrayal.
'... not only entertaining, but also holds up a mirror to the unfairness of zero hour contracts, greedy corporations and struggling families..' **** West End Wilma

My Mind is Free by Sam Hall
ISBN: 978-0-9926853-4-8 Paperback, 60pp, October 2015, £9.99
Four people wake up in the back of a truck and they have no idea how they got there. Nominated for the Human Trafficking Foundation's Anti-Slavery Day media awards 2016. *'...an engaging, challenging and powerful piece of theatre.'* Merton Against Trafficking

God's Waiting Room by Karen Bartholomew
ISBN: 978-0-9926853-5-5 Paperback, 48pp, June 2017, £9.99
Mother is dying slowly, the wait is unbearable, the pressures insurmountable, the thoughts unbelievable. Surely a gesture towards God's bigger plan is needed? Sisters Stella and Connie may be different from one another but share a common and profound love for their Mother. Can things really continue as they are?
"A brave, and moving piece of writing... Beautifully mixing laughs with unbearable pain."

Special offers on our website!

ISBN 978-0-9926853-6-2